ABOUT HABITATS
Rivers and Streams

To the One who created rivers and streams.
—*Genesis* 1:1

Published by
PEACHTREE PUBLISHING COMPANY INC.
1700 Chattahoochee Avenue
Atlanta, Georgia 30318-2112
PeachtreeBooks.com

Text © 2019 by Cathryn P. Sill
Illustrations © 2019 by John C. Sill

First trade paperback edition published in 2022

Edited by Vicky Holifield
Illustrations created in watercolor on archival quality 100% rag watercolor paper.

Printed and bound in March 2022 at Toppan Leefung, DongGuan, China.
10 9 8 7 6 5 4 3 2 1 (hardcover)
10 9 8 7 6 5 4 3 2 1 (trade paperback)
HC ISBN: 978-1-68263-091-4
PB ISBN: 978-1-68263-394-6

Library of Congress Cataloging-in-Publication Data
Names: Sill, Cathryn P., 1953– author. | Sill, John, illustrator. | Sill, Cathryn P., 1953– About
habitats.
Title: About habitats : rivers and streams / written by Cathryn Sill ; illustrated by John Sill.
Other titles: Rivers and streams
Description: First edition. | Atlanta, Georgia : Peachtree Publishing Company Inc., [2019] |
Series: About habitats | Audience: Ages 3–7. | Audience: K to grade 3.
Identifiers: LCCN 2018032021 | ISBN 9781682630914
Subjects: LCSH: Stream ecology—Juvenile literature. | Stream animals—Juvenile literature.
| Rivers—Juvenile literature.
Classification: LCC QH541.5.S7 S5725 2019 | DDC 577.6/4—dc23
LC record available at https://lccn.loc.gov/2018032021

ABOUT HABITATS
Rivers and Streams

Written by **Cathryn Sill**   Illustrated by **John Sill**

PEACHTREE
ATLANTA

PARTS OF A RIVER BASIN

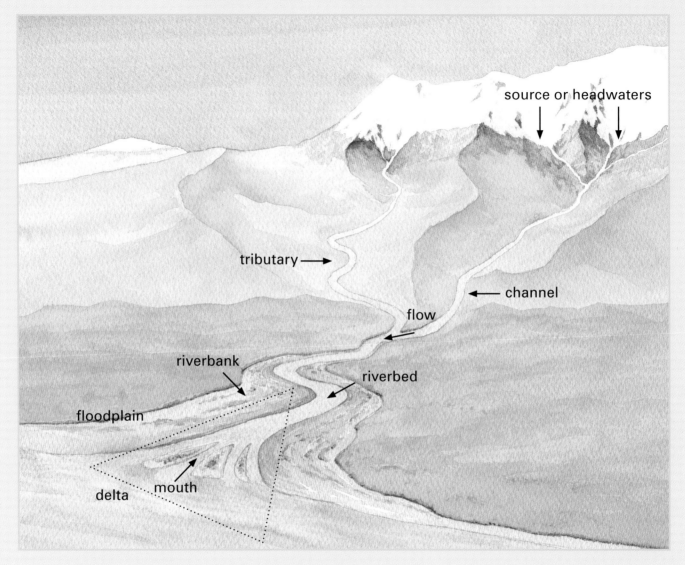

- source or headwaters—the beginning of a river
- tributary—a stream or river that flows into another river
- channel—the bed where a river flows
- riverbed—the bottom of a river
- flow—the water running in a river
- riverbank—the land along the edge of a river
- floodplain—the flat land next to a river that floods when the water is high
- mouth—the place where a river flows into another body of water, such as a lake or ocean
- delta—the land formed from sediment deposited at the mouth of a river

About Habitats
Rivers and Streams

Rivers and streams are places where fresh water flows across the land.

They are found in different habitats all over the world.

PLATE 2

a. **DESERT**
b. **TROPICAL RAINFOREST**
c. **TEMPERATE FOREST**
d. **TUNDRA**

b.

d.

Many rivers and streams start in mountains when water from rain and melting snow runs downhill.

Some rivers and streams begin when water from underground flows to the surface as a spring.

Small streams often join together to make larger streams and rivers that flow into oceans or lakes.

Some rivers become huge by the time they reach the ocean.

The water in mountain streams usually flows fast.

Rivers and streams flowing over high places and dropping to lower places create waterfalls.

When rivers flow through flat land, the water slows down.

Some rivers and streams dry up when there is no rain for a long time.

Storms, heavy rains, or a lot of melting snow can cause rivers to flood.

The fast-moving water in rivers is powerful and wears away the land.

Plants growing beside rivers help keep the riverbanks from washing away.

Rivers provide food and shelter for many kinds of animals.

PLATE 14
ALTAMAHA RIVER

Belted Kingfisher
Common Whitetail
North American River Otter
Spiny Softshell Turtle
Largemouth Bass
Great Egret
American Alligator

People need rivers for drinking water, electricity, food, transportation, and recreation.

a.

b.

c.

d.

e.

Polluted rivers and streams are harmful
to people and animals.

PLATE 16
OHIO RIVER

Rivers and streams are important places that need to be protected.

Rivers and Streams

Afterword

PLATE 1

Less than 3 percent of Earth's water is fresh (not salty). A tiny part of this fresh water is carried from one place to another in rivers and streams. Small rivers and streams are known by many names, including "creek," "branch," and "brook." The words "river" and "stream" are sometimes interchangeable, but people generally use the word "river" to refer to a larger stream of water. The Rio Grande flows about 1,900 miles (3,060 kilometers) through parts of southwestern United States and northern Mexico. Vermilion Flycatchers are fairly common along parts of the Rio Grande.

PLATE 2

Rivers around the world have some things in common. For example, they all have a source, a channel, and a mouth. But no two rivers are exactly alike because the land they flow through is different. Rivers flow through many areas such as rainforests, dry deserts, cold places like tundra, and temperate regions with four seasons.

PLATE 3

The beginning of a river is called its headwaters or source. Water from rain and melting snow creates rivers and streams as it flows across the land and drains into cracks in rocks and into low places such as gullies or ditches. Alpine Marmots, burrowing rodents that are members of the squirrel family, are found in the mountains of central and southern Europe.

PLATE 4

About 30 percent of Earth's fresh water is under the ground. Some water from rain and melting snow soaks into cracks in the rocks and small spaces in the soil. A spring is formed when water flows to the surface from underground. Spring Salamanders live in cool springs and streams in the Appalachian Mountains and other parts of the northeastern United States.

PLATE 5

A stream that flows into a larger stream or river is called a "tributary." Most rivers start out small and grow larger as tributaries join them. The larger river is called the "parent river" or "mainstem." The parent river and its tributaries make up a river system. Large rivers may have hundreds of tributaries.

PLATE 6

The biggest rivers may be miles wide and thousands of miles long and carry millions of gallons of water. More water flows into the ocean from the Amazon River in South America than from any other river. It is one of the longest rivers in the world. The Amazon can be up to 24.8 miles (40 kilometers) wide during the rainy season. Amazon River Dolphins (also known as Pink River Dolphins) are among the many animals that live in the huge Amazon River basin.

PLATE 7

Water rushes down the steep slopes of mountains. Some fish that live in fast water hunt behind rocks that shelter them from the strong current, but other animals don't need to avoid the fast-flowing water. Torrent Ducks are able to swim and dive in rushing water to search for food. They have strong, powerful claws on their feet that help them cling to slippery rocks. Torrent Ducks live in the Andes Mountains in South America.

PLATE 8

Waterfalls may plunge from high cliffs or cascade more gradually over a series of rocky steps. Some waterfalls have both steep drops and smaller cascades. Waterfalls can be very small, but some are quite large. Victoria Falls in southern Africa is one of the largest waterfalls in the world.

PLATE 9

Rivers in flat land often have many curves called "meanders." As river water slows down, it flows around rocks and bumps instead of rushing over them. The sideways movement of the water cuts into the land, causing the river to wind and bend. The Murray River is Australia's longest river. It starts in the Australian Alps, then meanders across flat land until it drains into the Southern Ocean. Australian Pelicans are common in Australia.

PLATE 10

Streams that stop flowing part of the time are called "temporary streams." They are common in arid (dry) lands. Temporary streams are important parts of a river system. They help protect the land from floods, add to the groundwater, and provide places for plants and animals to live. Sometimes rivers dry up because people take too much water from them. Collared Peccaries live in the southwestern United States and in parts of Central and South America.

PLATE 11

The area that floods when a river overflows its banks is called the floodplain. Floods can help people by depositing nutrients in the ground. Floodplains often have rich soil and are good places to raise crops. When people live in floodplains or too close to rivers, floods may destroy their property. Millions of people worldwide have lost their homes in floods.

PLATE 12

Rivers can wear away land and create new land. The process that wears the earth away is called "erosion." Erosion occurs along rivers and streams. As a stream flows quickly, it picks up and carries sediment—soil, sand, and rocks. The fast-flowing water bearing the sediment causes erosion. Then, as the stream slows down, it drops or deposits the sediment. The deposits build up over time and make new land. Erosion sometimes forms deep river valleys or canyons. Desert Bighorn Sheep live on the steep slopes of canyons and mountains in the southwestern United States and in northwestern Mexico.

PLATE 13

Erosion along rivers becomes a problem when plants are removed from the banks. Roots of plants hold the soil in place. Without plants, the banks wash away and large amounts of sediment flow into the stream. Too much sediment in streams harms the animals and plants that live there. Black Phoebes are found along streams in western United States, Central America, and parts of South America.

PLATE 14

Rivers around the world provide homes for all kinds of animals, including fish, insects, reptiles, amphibians, crustaceans, mollusks, mammals, and birds. Some animals live in rivers all the time. Other animals that live on land depend on rivers for fresh water to drink and a place to hunt for food. The Altamaha River, located in the southeastern United States, supports many animals, including several species that are endangered.

PLATE 15

Throughout history people have depended on rivers and streams for survival. Many major towns and cities are located along rivers. Some activities of these communities can cause damage that harms river habitats. Waterways should be protected so that all the people and wildlife that depend on them can continue to use them safely.

PLATE 16

Rivers become polluted when harmful substances such as sewage, garbage, or toxic chemicals are dumped in them. When people or animals drink the dirty water from polluted rivers, they may get diseases. Eating fish from polluted water can also make people and animals sick. In some places laws prevent people from polluting rivers. In other places there are no laws to protect rivers. Partly because of the many factories and coal plants along the Ohio River, it is one of the dirtiest rivers in the United States.

PLATE 17

Healthy rivers are necessary to people and the animals and plants that live in or near them. Fortunately, damage to rivers can often be repaired. Several years ago the River Thames in southern England was so polluted that very few animals could live in it. Plans were made to clean up the river and laws were passed to protect it. The River Thames is now one of the world's cleanest rivers that flows through a major city. Mute Swans are native to Eurasia and northern Africa. They have been introduced to North America.

GLOSSARY

BIOME—an area such as a forest or a wetland that shares the same types of plants and animals
ECOSYSTEM—a community of living things and their environment
HABITAT—the place where animals and plants live

current—the flow of a moving body of water
endangered—threatened with becoming extinct
groundwater—water within the earth that supplies springs and wells
gully—a ditch made by flowing water
river—a natural course of moving water, usually of substantial size
river basin—the area of land drained by a river and its tributaries
current—the flow in a moving body of water
stream—a moving body of water of any size
temperate—not very hot and not very cold
toxic—poisonous
tundra—a large treeless area where the underground soil stays frozen

BIBLIOGRAPHY

BOOKS

ENDANGERED RIVERS: INVESTIGATING RIVERS IN CRISIS by Rani Iyer (Capstone Press).
IT'S ALL ABOUT… RUSHING RIVERS by Editors of Kingfisher (Kingfisher Books).
RIVERS, LAKES, STREAMS, AND PONDS (Biomes Atlases) by Richard Beatty (Raintree).

WEBSITES

"Nature Works," *www.nhptv.org/natureworks/nwep7j.htm*
"National Geographic," *www.nationalgeographic.org/encyclopedia/river*
"International Rivers," *www.internationalrivers.org/healthy-rivers*

ABOUT... SERIES

HC: 978-1-68263-031-0
PB: 978-1-68263-032-7

HC: 978-1-56145-038-1
PB: 978-1-56145-364-1

HC: 978-1-56145-688-8
PB: 978-1-56145-699-4

HC: 978-1-56145-301-6
PB: 978-1-56145-405-1

HC: 978-1-56145-987-2
PB: 978-1-56145-988-9

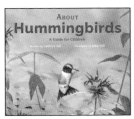

HC: 978-1-56145-588-1
PB: 978-1-56145-837-0

HC: 978-1-56145-881-3
PB: 978-1-56145-882-0

HC: 978-1-56145-757-1
PB: 978-1-56145-758-8

HC: 978-1-56145-906-3
PB: 978-1-68263-288-8

HC: 978-1-56145-358-0
PB: 978-1-56145-407-5

PB: 978-1-56145-406-8

HC: 978-1-56145-795-3
PB: 978-1-68263-158-4

HC: 978-1-56145-743-4
PB: 978-1-56145-741-0

HC: 978-1-56145-536-2
PB: 978-1-56145-811-0

HC: 978-1-56145-907-0
PB: 978-1-56145-908-7

HC: 978-1-56145-454-9
PB: 978-1-56145-914-8

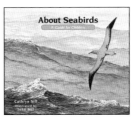

HC: 978-1-68263-092-1

HC: 978-1-68263-234-5

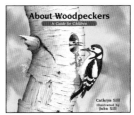

HC: 978-1-68263-004-4

ALSO AVAILABLE IN SPANISH
AND ENGLISH/SPANISH
EDITIONS

• About Amphibians / Sobre los anfibios PB: 978-1-68263-033-4 • Sobre los anfibios PB: 978-1-68263-230-7 • About Birds / Sobre los pájaros PB: 978-1-56145-783-0
• Sobre los pájaros PB: 978-1-68263-071-6 • About Fish / Sobre los peces PB: 978-1-56145-989-6 • Sobre los peces PB: 978-1-68263-154-6
• About Insects / Sobre los insectos PB: 978-1-56145-883-7 • Sobre los insectos PB: 978-1-68263-155-3 • About Mammals / Sobre los mamíferos PB: 978-1-56145-800-4
• Sobre los mamíferos PB: 978-1-68263-072-3 • About Reptiles / Sobre los reptiles PB: 978-1-56145-909-4 • Sobre los reptiles PB: 978-1-68263-231-4

ABOUT HABITATS SERIES

HC: 978-1-56145-641-3
PB: 978-1-56145-636-9

HC: 978-1-56145-734-2
PB: 978-1-68263-126-3

HC: 978-1-56145-559-1
PB: 978-1-68263-034-1

HC: 978-1-56145-469-3
PB: 978-1-56145-731-1

HC: 978-1-56145-618-5
PB: 978-1-56145-960-5

HC: 978-1-56145-832-5
PB: 978-1-68263-334-2

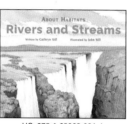

HC: 978-1-68263-091-4
PB: 978-1-68263-394-6

HC: 978-1-56145-968-1
PB: 978-1-68263-402-8

HC: 978-1-68263-233-8

HC: 978-1-56145-432-7
PB: 978-1-56145-689-5

THE SILLS

CATHRYN AND JOHN SILL are the talented team who created the *About…* series as well as the *About Habitats* series. Their books have garnered praise from educators and have won a variety of awards, including Bank Street Best Books, CCBC Choices, NSTA/CBC Outstanding Science Trade Books for Students K–12, Orbis Pictus Recommended, and *Science Books & Films* Best Books of the Year. Cathryn, a graduate of Western Carolina University, taught early elementary school classes for thirty years. John holds a BS in wildlife biology from North Carolina State University. Combining his artistic skill and knowledge of wildlife, he has achieved an impressive reputation as a wildlife artist. The Sills live in Franklin, North Carolina.

Fred Eldredge, Creative Image Photography